To Jenny, Jos,
Diana and Helen

First published 1989
by Walker Books Ltd
87 Vauxhall Walk
London SE11 5HJ

This edition published 1998

2 4 6 8 10 9 7 5 3 1

© 1989 Marcia Williams

Printed in Hong Kong

British Library Cataloguing in Publication Data
A catalogue record for this book is
available from the British Library.

ISBN 0-7445-6059-4

JONAH
AND THE WHALE

Written and illustrated by
Marcia Williams

WALKER BOOKS
AND SUBSIDIARIES

LONDON • BOSTON • SYDNEY

Many, many moons ago

in a land of deserts and date palms

God spoke to a man named Jonah.

"Arise," He said, "and go to Nineveh.

Warn the people against their wickedness,

for if they do not change their ways

I shall destroy their city."

But Jonah did not believe God would do this.

He decided to run away, and not go to Nineveh.

He found a ship travelling to Tarshish,

in the opposite direction from Nineveh.

He paid his fare and went on board.

This angered God,

so He sent a tempestuous storm.

The howling wind tore at the ship's sail.

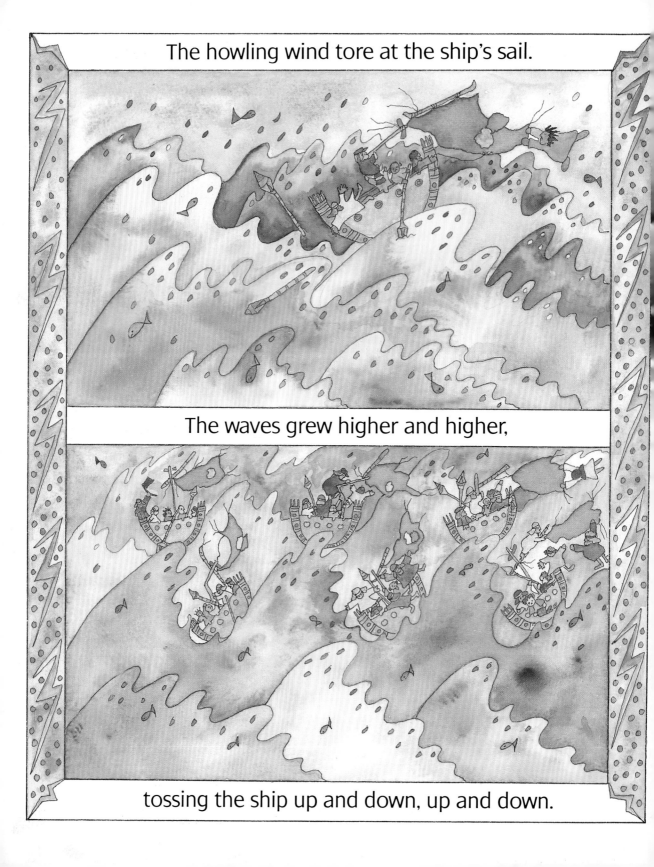

The waves grew higher and higher,

tossing the ship up and down, up and down.

The sailors feared that the ship would break in two.

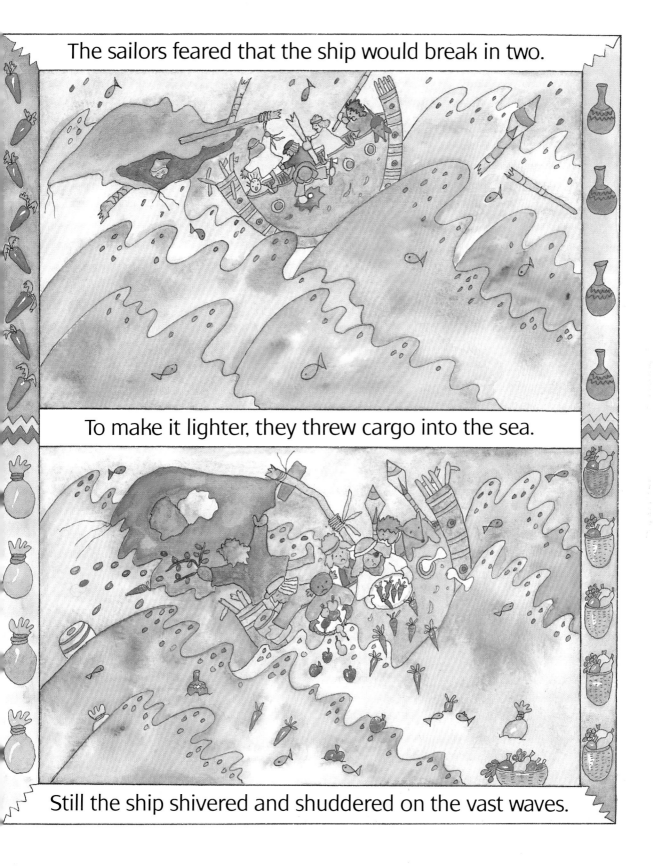

To make it lighter, they threw cargo into the sea.

Still the ship shivered and shuddered on the vast waves.

Above deck the sailors prayed to their gods

while below, Jonah slept

until the captain woke him.

"Jonah," he said, "pray to your God to save us!"

Though Jonah prayed, the storm grew even fiercer.

The sailors and their captain were terrified.

Then Jonah told them that God had sent the storm

because he had not gone to Nineveh.

"If I give myself to the sea," said Jonah,

"I'm sure the waters will be calm again."

The sailors did not want Jonah to drown

and they tried hard to row to land.

But in vain, for the sea became even wilder.

So, sadly, they threw Jonah overboard.

Instantly the raging waters grew calm.

Fearing for Jonah's life,

the sailors prayed to God for forgiveness.

Then they set sail again for Tarshish

on the still, clear waters.

But Jonah did not drown.

At first he floated.

Then he became caught in weeds.

Jonah was dragged

into the depths of the sea.

Just as he felt he was about to die,

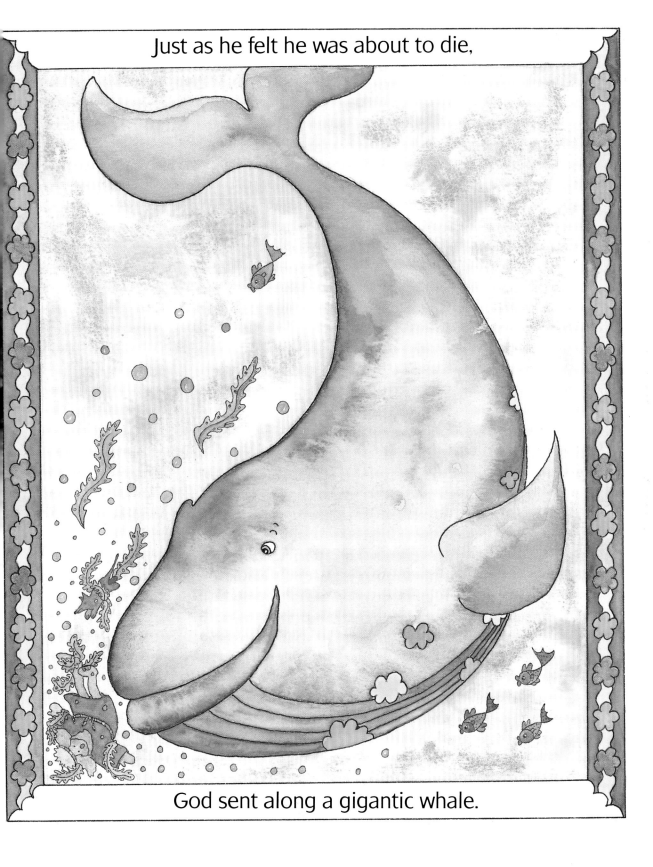

God sent along a gigantic whale.

The whale swallowed Jonah whole.

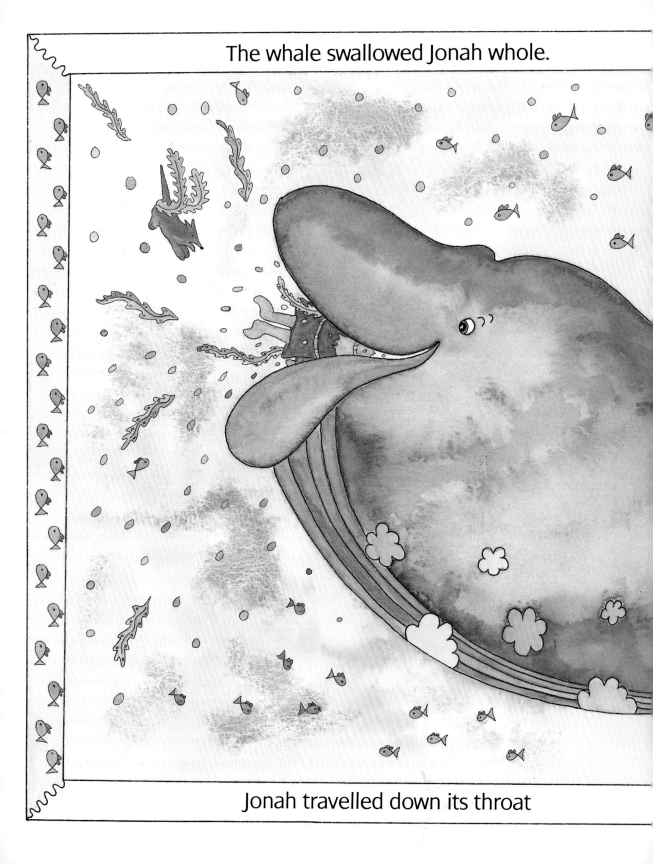

Jonah travelled down its throat

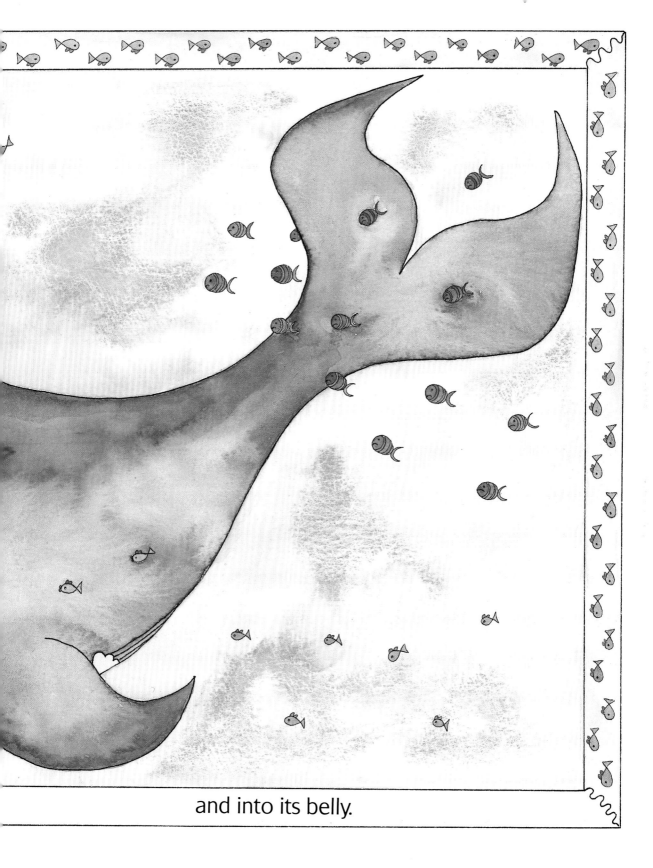

and into its belly.

It was cold and dark and Jonah was afraid.

Three days and three nights passed.

Sometimes Jonah slept,

but mostly he prayed to God to forgive him.

At last God took pity on Jonah

and told the whale to spit him out.

Jonah landed on the earth with a bump.

He was very shaken

and could hardly stand on his feet,

but he was glad to be on dry land.

Then God spoke to Jonah again.

"Go to Nineveh," He said, "and warn the people

that in forty days their city will be destroyed

unless they become good and kind."

This time Jonah obeyed God.

He travelled to Nineveh and cried out God's warning.

The King and people of Nineveh believed Jonah.

They put on sackcloth and promised to repent.

When God saw this he was happy to spare them,

and Jonah and everyone who lived in Nineveh rejoiced.

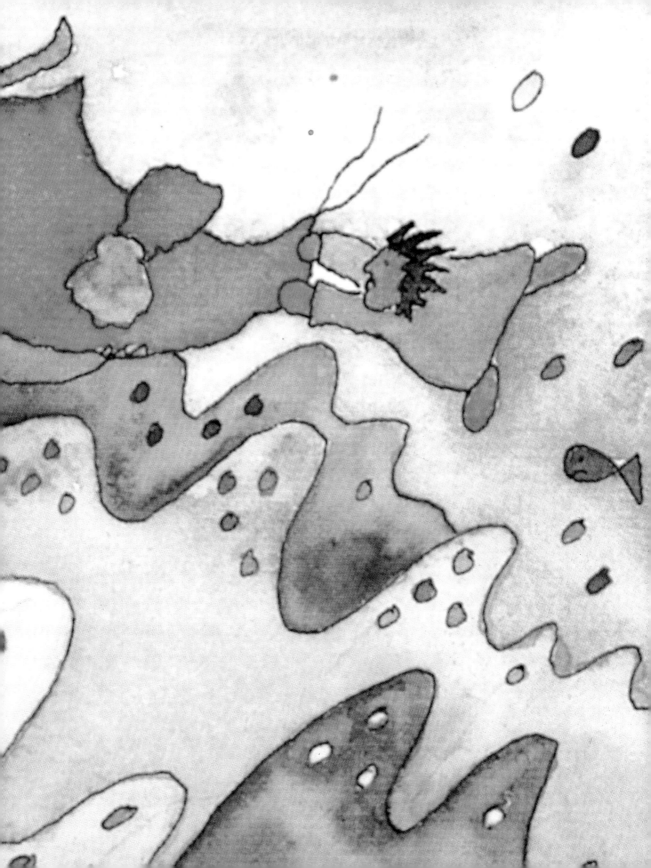

MORE WALKER PAPERBACKS
For You to Enjoy

Other retellings by Marcia Williams

THE AMAZING STORY OF NOAH'S ARK

The amazing story of Noah and his ark is one of the world's greatest and best-loved tales.
Bright comic-strip illustrations and a simple text bring this favourite
Old Testament story to life for young children.

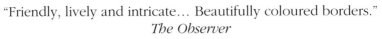

"Friendly, lively and intricate… Beautifully coloured borders."
The Observer

0-7445-6058-6   £4.99

JOSEPH AND HIS MAGNIFICENT COAT OF MANY COLOURS

Full of drama, incident and emotion, the adventures of Joseph are as
colourful as his glorious coat itself.

"Every page is awash with colour and detail…
Children will find much to enjoy here." *Child Education*

0-7445-6060-8   £4.99

THE ILIAD AND THE ODYSSEY

The Iliad tells the story of the war between the Greeks and the Trojans.
The Odyssey depicts the perilous voyage home of the Greek warrior, Odysseus.

"A big, beautifully produced book, telling the stories in irresistibly detailed
comic-strip form… Elegant, intelligent, funny, dramatic and totally absorbing;
the perfect start to an early familiarity with Homer." *The Guardian*

0-7445-5430-6   £5.99